Lacy Sunshine's
Wonderland
Coloring Book Volume 11

Illustrated by
Heather Valentin

©Heather Valentin. Lacy Sunshine. All Rights Reserved.
Personal Use Only. No Redistribution. No Sharing Or Posting Of These
Uncolored Images Anywhere Including But Not Limitesd Too
Social Media Sites.

Made in United States
Troutdale, OR
08/10/2024